'TWAS A DARK AND STORMY NIGHT...

WHY WRITERS WRITE

Library of Congress Cataloging-in-Publication Data

Murray, Jennifer.
   'Twas a dark and stormy night ... -- : why writers write / by Jennifer Murray.
      p. cm. -- (Shockwave)
      Includes index.
   ISBN-10: 0-531-17773-4 (lib. bdg.)
   ISBN-13: 978-0-531-17773-0 (lib. bdg.)
   ISBN-10: 0-531-15543-9 (pbk.)
   ISBN-13: 978-0-531-15543-1 (pbk.)

 1. Children's literature--Authorship--Juvenile literature. 2. Authorship
--Juvenile literature. I. Title.

   PN147.5.M88 2008
   808.06'8--dc22

2007016734

Published in 2008 by Children's Press, an imprint of Scholastic Inc.,
557 Broadway, New York, New York 10012
www.scholastic.com

SCHOLASTIC, CHILDREN'S PRESS, and associated logos are trademarks
and/or registered trademarks of Scholastic Inc.

08 09 10 11 12 13 14 15 16 17
10 9 8 7 6 5 4 3 2 1

Printed in China through Colorcraft Ltd., Hong Kong

Author: Jennifer Murray
Educational Consultant: Ian Morrison
Editor: Jennifer Murray
Designer: Avon Willis
Photo Researcher: Sarah Matthewson

Photographs by: Big Stock Photo (page, quill and inkpot, typewriter, laptop, pp. 8–9; quill and inkpot, p. 11; looking
glass globe, p. 12; chocolate bar, p. 13, p. 34); **Getty Images** (Sandra Cisneros, p. 15; p. 18; Maurice Sendak, p. 26;
The Cat in the Hat, p. 27); **The Granger Collection, New York** (*Huckleberry Finn*, p. 10; *To Kill a Mockingbird*, p. 16;
Little Women, p. 28; Louisa Alcott, p. 29; Charles Dodgson, p. 29); **Jennifer and Brian Lupton** (teenagers, pp. 32–33);
Macmillan Publishers Ltd, London, UK: Copyright © 1998, cover photography by Jutta Klee (cover of *Are You There
God? It's Me, Margaret* by Judy Blume, p. 16); Copyright © 1997, cover design by Black Sheep (cover of *Kiss the Dust*
by Elizabeth Laird, p. 25); **More Images/North Wind Picture Archives** (Mark Twain, p. 10); **Penguin Books Ltd.:**
Front cover of *Charlie and the Chocolate Factory* by Roald Dahl and illustrated by Quentin Blake (Puffin Books, 2005).
Text copyright © Roald Dahl Nominee Ltd, 1964. Illustrations copyright © Quentin Blake, 1995, 1997. Reproduced
by permission of Penguin Books Ltd. (*Charlie and the Chocolate Factory*, p. 13); **Photolibrary** (cover; book bag, p. 9;
Harry Potter, p. 12; "The Mad Hatter's Tea Party," p. 14; Helen Keller, p. 17; *Oliver Twist* cover, p. 19; *The Lion, the
Witch, and the Wardrobe*, map, p. 20; p. 22; *Red Riding Hood*, Shakespeare, p. 23; p. 24; *Sherlock Holmes*, p. 25;
Lord of the Rings, pp. 32–33); **The Random House Group Ltd, UK.** Reprinted by permission (cover of *Beloved* by Toni
Morrison, p. 13); **Stock Central/TopFoto:** (Frankenstein, pp. 20–21); ©2003 Topham Picturepoint (*Lord of the Rings*,
p. 15); **Tranz: Camera Press** (Judy Blume, p. 16; Toni Morrison, p. 13); **Corbis** (p. 3; p. 7; Christopher Paolini, p. 11;
J. K. Rowling, p. 12; Alice Liddell, p. 14; Charles Dickens, workhouse scene from *Oliver Twist*, p. 19; Amazing Stories,
p. 21; Kamisibai storytelling, p. 21; *Pied Piper*, p. 23; Peter Pan, p. 26; Dr. Seuss, p. 27; Lemony Snicket, p. 28; George
Eliot, Count Olaf, p. 29); **Zuma** (*Eragon* movie-still, p. 11)

All illustrations and other photographs © Weldon Owen Education Inc.

SHOCKWAVE
SOCIAL STUDIES

'Twas a Dark and Stormy Night...

WHY WRITERS WRITE

❦ JENNIFER MURRAY ❧

children's press®

An imprint of Scholastic Inc.

NEW YORK • TORONTO • LONDON • AUCKLAND • SYDNEY
MEXICO CITY • NEW DELHI • HONG KONG
DANBURY, CONNECTICUT

CHECK THESE OUT!

SHOCKER
Stuff to Shock, Surprise, and Amaze You

Quick Recaps and Notable Notes

Word Stunners and Other Oddities

The Heads-Up on Expert Reading

Links to More Information

CONTENTS

autobiography (*aw toh bye OG ruh fee*) a book in which the author tells the story of his or her life

illusion (*i LOO zhuhn*) something that appears to exist but does not

manuscript (*MAN yuh skript*) the original typed or handwritten version of a book or a piece of music before it is printed

plagiarism (*PLAY juh riz um*) the stealing of another person's ideas and presenting them as your own

protagonist (*proh TAG uh nist*) the leading character in a story

pseudonym (*SOOD uh nim*) a false name, especially one used by an author instead of his or her real name

For additional vocabulary, see Glossary on page 34.

The prefix *auto-* in *autobiography* means "self" or "on one's own." Related words include *autograph*, *automobile*, and *automatic*.

Jean Meliot, a writer in the fifteenth century, is working on a manuscript.

Why do writers write? Some writers seek fame and fortune through their books. Other writers want to share their knowledge. They write **nonfiction** books that teach us about subjects such as science or history. Other writers write about their own experiences. They may write a journal, a memoir, or an **autobiography**.

This is a nonfiction book that explores the subject of writing. The main focus of this book is fiction. Writers of fiction create imaginary people, worlds, and events. Some stories are entertaining. Some have a serious message. Some works of fiction are based on actual events. The writer uses facts as a starting point to create fiction that departs from those facts. Other fiction is based completely on fantasy or imagination.

All kinds of books, whether fiction or nonfiction, can open windows to new ideas and experiences.

Time Line of Inventions for Writing

3000 B.C.	500–1400 A.D.
About 3000 B.C., the ancient Egyptians used papyrus plant reeds to make a material they could write on. They wrote with brushes made from reeds. The word *paper* comes from the Egyptian word *papyrus*.	Between 500 and 1400 A.D., books were written by hand. Scribes copied the text on **parchment**. The writing of a single book took about a year to complete.

1400s	**1900s**	**Today**
The invention of the printing press by Johannes Gutenberg in Germany meant books could be produced quickly and far more cheaply. The first book printed by Gutenberg's press was a Latin Bible in 1455.	Christopher Latham Sholes and two colleagues invented the first commercially successful typewriter. It was **patented** in 1868. The typewriter would eventually lead to the development of the word processor a century later.	Today, writers can write anywhere in the world. Laptop computers are portable. Voice recognition technology means that writers don't even have to type! They can **dictate** their text instead.

9

Why Do Writers Write?

Some writers hope their writing will help make things better. A work of fiction or nonfiction can be powerful in changing the way people think. Expressing beliefs, opinions, and ideas is an important part of writing. Writers often document and help preserve the culture and customs of their country through their work.

If a piece of writing is translated into other languages, it can have worldwide impact. Periods of history are remembered through the writing of people who lived at that time.

Mark Twain

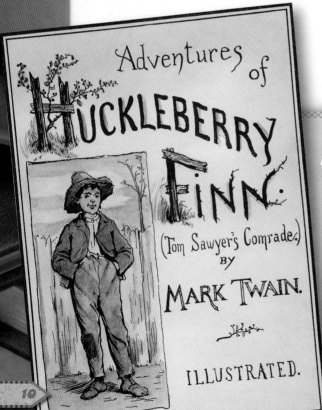

Adventures of HUCKLEBERRY FINN. (Tom Sawyer's Comrade.) BY MARK TWAIN. ILLUSTRATED.

Sometimes authors can be taken by surprise. Mark Twain wrote *Adventures of Huckleberry Finn* for adult readers. However, the story of a young boy named Huck and his adventures on the Mississippi River has become a classic story for children.

Most published authors are adults. However, Christopher Paolini was only nineteen when his story *Eragon* was published. *Eragon* is about a fifteen-year-old boy who is a dragon rider. Paolini wrote his original **manuscript** of *Eragon* in **calligraphy**, using pen and ink.

Christopher Paolini's characters and stories were brought to life in the movie based on his book. ▼

Writers write in order to …

- change the way people think
- express ideas and beliefs
- preserve culture and customs

Book Ingredient: GENRE

Books can be divided into different groups. These literary groups are known as genres. Nonfiction is a big genre that includes all fact-based books. Fiction is also a big genre. It is made up of many other genres. These include adventure, fantasy, romance, science fiction, drama, and comedy.

Through the Looking Glass

INSPIRATION

Where do writers get their ideas? Did a real Alice inspire *Alice in Wonderland*? Is there really a house on Mango Street? What inspired Charlie's visit to a chocolate factory? The smallest event in real life can lead an author's imagination in any direction. The reader is often left wondering where reality ends and fiction begins.

J. K. Rowling was stuck on a train for four hours. She sat waiting and daydreaming. The idea of a young boy learning to become a wizard just popped into her head. As soon as she got home, she started writing. The result was *Harry Potter and the Sorcerer's Stone*.

The Harry Potter books are read by adults and children. They have been published in two different covers. One has a colorful illustration for children. The other has a black-and-white photo to make it look more serious for adult readers!

I recognize most of the authors' names and book titles on these pages. Having some background knowledge makes reading more interesting.

▶ When Roald Dahl was at school in England, the chocolate company Cadbury sent boxes of new sweets and chocolates to his school for the pupils to test. The young Roald dreamt of sending the recipe for a new chocolate bar directly to Mr. Cadbury himself. He never did create a new bar, but the idea inspired him to invent Willy Wonka's strange and enchanting chocolate factory in *Charlie and the Chocolate Factory*.

◀ Toni Morrison draws on her experiences as an African-American female in the twentieth and twenty-first centuries. She writes about the lives of African Americans. Her **novels**, such as *Beloved* and *The Bluest Eye*, deal with the history of African-American people, and the problems they face in America today.

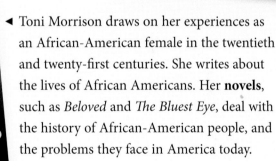

Book Ingredient: SETTING

This is one of the most important things when writing a book. The writer must set the scene so that the reader has all the details needed to understand the place and time in which the story occurs. This includes creating an appropriate atmosphere.

FACT AND FICTION

Facts are what happens in real life. Fiction is made up in a writer's imagination. But fiction can create an **illusion** of reality, and occasionally, fiction starts out as facts. Sometimes writers **distort** reality until the real people and places are unrecognizable in their books. They might do this by changing the names, or altering the details. Some elements of the setting might remain true to life.

One sunny afternoon, a writer named Lewis Carroll told a story to a ten-year-old girl named Alice Liddell and her sisters. The girls loved it, and asked him to write it down for them. In 1865, the story was published as *Alice's Adventures in Wonderland*. It was so popular that Lewis Carroll wrote a companion story called *Through the Looking Glass*.

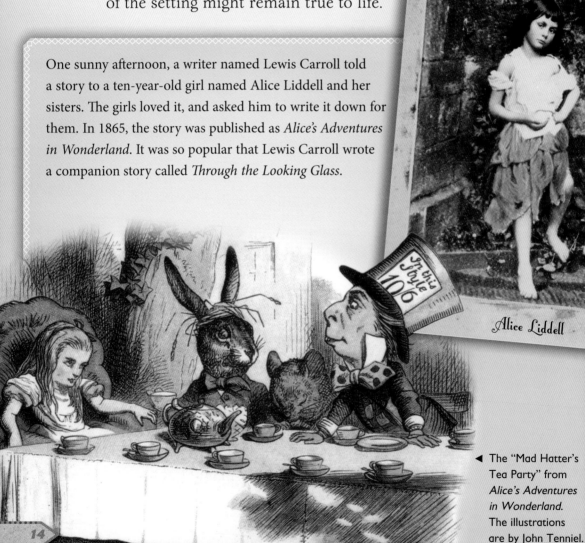

Alice Liddell

◀ The "Mad Hatter's Tea Party" from *Alice's Adventures in Wonderland*. The illustrations are by John Tenniel.

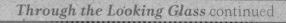

◄ The Lord of the Rings **trilogy** and *The Hobbit* were written by J. R. R. Tolkien. Tolkien was born in South Africa. At the age of three, he moved to England. His aunt had a house called Bag End. This later became the name of the home of Bilbo and Frodo Baggins, the main characters in Tolkien's books.

The House on Mango Street was written ► by Sandra Cisneros. The house in the story is owned by the Cordero family, and it is in Chicago. Like the main character in her story, Esperanza Cordero, Sandra Cisneros grew up in a house in Chicago.

Book Ingredient: THE PLOT

The plot is the story line that runs through the book. Most plots have a beginning, a middle, and an end. The beginning introduces the characters. The middle often has twists and turns to keep the reader guessing what will happen. The end ties up everything that has happened so that it makes sense to the reader.

Now I get it! This is the third time the "Book Ingredient" has appeared at the bottom of the page. This must be an ongoing feature. I'll look for more examples as I continue reading the book.

CROSSING THE LINE

When writers base a work of fiction on the lives of real people, they must be careful. If the real people are able to recognize themselves in the fictional characters, they may be offended. They can even take legal action for **slander**.

Fiction often crosses the line from the invented world into the real world. The writer may decide to do this if he or she has an important message to express to the reader.

◄ Judy Blume writes about **controversial** subjects. Her books are about the problems some young people encounter growing up. Some of her books have been banned in schools and libraries because they are too shocking. One of her most widely read books is *Are You There God? It's Me, Margaret*.

► *To Kill a Mockingbird* by Harper Lee deals with problems of race in the southern United States in the early twentieth century. It is a powerful story that crosses many lines between fact and fiction. The main female character is very like the author. Harper Lee grew up in Monroeville, Alabama, which provides the setting for the town in the story. Her father was a lawyer. As a child, Harper was aware of controversial and unpopular court cases. These memories formed the basis of her story.

Judy Blume

Deaf and blind from an early age, Helen Keller was an extraordinary writer. Born in 1880, Helen learned to read using **Braille**. However, her early career as a writer was plagued by scandal. At the age of eleven, Helen wrote *The Frost King*. But her story was so like another story named *The Frost Fairies* by Margaret T. Canby that Helen was accused of **plagiarism**. The case went to court. Helen pleaded that she had not realized what she was doing. The judge believed her claim that she had mistaken a memory of reading *The Frost Fairies* for true inspiration.

Helen Keller

Book Ingredient: CHARACTER

The hero, or **protagonist**, is the main character in the book. The actions of the protagonist are often followed over the course of the story. The development of this character can be as important and as interesting as the plot. If the writer has created a realistic character, the reader can identify with the protagonist. This means that the reader understands, likes, or recognizes elements of the protagonist's personality. While reading the book, the reader might feel supportive, sympathetic, scared, happy, or many other things in regard to the character.

Into Another World

Reading fiction or a **biography** can take the reader into the life of another person. A writer sometimes describes the events of his or her own life in an autobiography, memoir, or diary.

During World War II, Anne Frank used her diary to record her thoughts, frustrations, and daily life during the two years she spent in hiding. *The Diary of a Young Girl* records details that are familiar to young people today. Anne fights with her sister, struggles with lessons, and is bored with her confined life. The world events going on in the background make the diary historically important. Anne and her family were Jewish. They fled Germany in the 1930s when Adolf Hitler's Nazi party began a campaign against the Jewish people. When World War II began in 1939, the Franks went into hiding in Amsterdam, Netherlands. They hid in a secret **annex** of rooms for two years until they were betrayed. Anne died in a Nazi concentration camp when she was only fifteen years old.

Anne Frank

The word *diary* comes from the Latin *diarium* meaning "daily allowance." A journal, which is similar to a diary, is related to the French word *jour* meaning "day."

The details and characters in Charles Dickens's novels paint a picture of what life was like in nineteenth-century England. Dickens wrote about all kinds of people, rich and poor, good and bad. Many of his characters struggle to live in difficult conditions. In *Oliver Twist*, an orphan – Oliver – grows up in a workhouse where he is badly treated. This was a reality for many children during the nineteenth century. Dickens revealed the social problems of the time by writing about them as fiction.

▼ Illustration from *Oliver Twist* by Charles Dickens

"Bumble refuses more porridge to the Workhouse boys."
(OLIVER TWIST)

Book Ingredient: THE NARRATOR

The narrator is the person who is telling the story. If the narrator is also the main character in the story, it is said to be written in the "first person." This can give the reader a direct insight into thoughts and opinions of the main character. If the narrator is describing what is happening, but is not one of the characters in the story, then it is said to be written in the "third person." This can distance the reader from knowing one character intimately and feeling involved in the story. However, it can allow the reader to know more about the other characters, and to have a less biased view of the story.

FANTASY AND SCIENCE

Fantasy and science fiction are genres in which writers create completely new worlds as the setting for their stories. Science fiction is based on real or imagined progress in science or technology. Both fantasy and science fiction can include characters that are not human. The world created by the author may be very strange to the reader. If their writing is to be convincing, the author has to explain how this new world works. The Chronicles of Narnia by C. S. Lewis are fantasy stories for children. Narnia is a magical place that the characters can enter from the real world.

In *The Lion, the Witch, and the Wardrobe* by C. S. Lewis, the main characters enter the world of Narnia through a wardrobe. ▶

Fantasy and Science Fiction
- both are fiction
- highly entertaining
- create new worlds
- nonhuman characters
- science or magic theme

◀ J. R. R. Tolkien's The Lord of the Rings is one of the most famous series of books set in a fantasy world. Tolkien even created languages spoken by the inhabitants of his fantasy world. He also drew detailed maps of the lands in which the books are set.

FICTION

Many science fiction books are set in space. Some have included robots, time travel, and aliens. The world created in science fiction often seems to be scientifically possible. Mary Shelley's *Frankenstein* (1818) is considered to be the first science fiction novel. It is the story of Dr. Frankenstein, a scientist who tries to create a perfect being, but instead creates a monster. Mary Shelley's novel is relevant today as it deals with the problem of how far science should go in creating and molding human beings. The issue of **cloning** is a related and real-life debate.

◄ This illustration shows Dr. Frankenstein and his creation. The creature is human-like in appearance, but is rejected by society. He then acts monstrously in revenge.

SHOCKER

The science fiction novel *The War of the Worlds* by H. G. Wells was first read on radio in America in 1938. Hundreds of people thought it was a real news story about aliens landing!

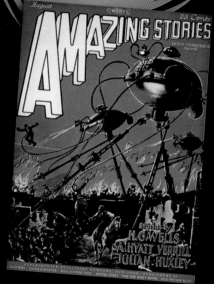

▲ Science fiction magazines grew in popularity during the twentieth century. *The War of the Worlds* by H. G. Wells was first published in a magazine.

Tell Me a Story

Long before stories were written down, or published in books, they were told aloud. These stories included **myths**, **fables**, and **folktales**. This is an important part of the development of literature. In twelfth-century Japan, storytellers told stories using pictures on paper scrolls. This storytelling was called *kamishibai*. It continues today.

Once Upon a Time...

Fiction and nonfiction are as old as human society. From cave paintings to e-books, people have passed on stories and knowledge. The history of literature reflects the influences and pressures on writers through the ages. Over 600 years ago, texts were extremely rare. They were written by hand. Many of them retold religious stories.

The **Renaissance** in Europe changed literature forever. In the 1400s, Johannes Gutenberg invented the printing press. Texts could now be produced cheaply and in large numbers. The earliest printed texts included the Bible in Latin. The first texts to be printed in English were a collection of stories about King Arthur (an English legend), and *The Canterbury Tales* by Geoffrey Chaucer.

◀ Illustration from Chaucer's *The Canterbury Tales*

▼ Page from Gutenberg's printed Bible

SHOCKER

Geoffrey Chaucer was also a spy and diplomat. After 1400, his name disappears from all records. Rumor suggests he was murdered while on a mission!

Plays and performances were popular during the Renaissance. Many theaters were built. **Playwrights** wrote history plays, comedies, and tragedies. One of the most successful playwrights at this time was William Shakespeare.

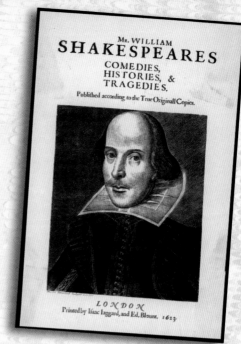

◀ Little Red Riding Hood

▶ The Pied Piper

Fairy tales are among the oldest stories. They began as folktales. They were spoken by storytellers. The tales were for adults as well as children. Eventually, fairy tales were collected and written down. One of the most famous collections was written by the Brothers Grimm. They lived in Germany during the 1800s. Since then, stories such as "Little Red Riding Hood," "The Pied Piper," and "Cinderella" have been retold again and again. Hans Christian Andersen, a Danish writer, was inspired by fairy tales. In the late 1800s, he created his own stories based on some of the tales. These include "The Ugly Duckling" and "The Emperor's New Clothes."

The novel is the most common form of fiction today. However, it did not appear until the early eighteenth century. One of the first novelists was Daniel Defoe. He wrote *Robinson Crusoe* in 1719.

As well as novelists, playwrights, and poets, there were many political **pamphleteers**. Their pamphlets were not fiction. They were short texts on political issues. The writers criticized the way things were. They tried to bring about change. The pamphlets were given out to many people in the hope of influencing government decisions. Jonathan Swift, who wrote the novel *Gulliver's Travels*, was also a pamphleteer.

Gulliver's Travels ▶

Jonathan Swift

Book Ingredient: CHAPTERS

Sometimes longer stories are divided into sections called chapters. Chapters often have titles of their own. This allows the author the freedom to switch between different settings, times, and events. The start of a new chapter, and the chapter's title, can alert the reader to something new, without much explanation in the text.

HE STRAND MAGAZINE

DECEMBER, 1911.   No. 252.

A NEW ADVENTURE OF

Sherlock Holmes.

e Disappearance of Lady Frances Carfax.

By ARTHUR CONAN DOYLE.

Illustrated by Alec Ball.

UT why Turkish?" asked Mr. Sherlock Holmes, gazing fixedly at my boots. I was reclining in a cane-backed chair at the moment, and my protruded feet had attracted his ever - active tion.
English," I answered, in some surprise. ot them at Latimer's, in Oxford Street."

" Bravo, Watson ! A very dignified and logical remonstrance. Let me see, what were the points? Take the last one first—the cab. You observe that you have some splashes on the left sleeve and shoulder of your coat. Had you sat in the centre of a hansom you would probably have had no splashes, and if you had they would certainly have been symmetrical. Therefore it is clear that you sat at the side. Therefore it is equally clear

In the nineteenth century, magazines began to publish short stories. They also published longer stories as serials. Many novels by Charles Dickens were originally published as installments in magazines. The adventures of the fictional detective Sherlock Holmes, by Arthur Conan Doyle, also first appeared as serials. In the United States, similar magazines featured cowboys and other heroes and villains of the Wild West.

Throughout history, writers have dealt with the problems of their time and described the world around them. Fiction in the twentieth century also reflected great world events, such as World Wars I and II, the Vietnam War, and conflicts in the Middle East, Africa, and Asia. Many people wrote about their experiences during these real wars. They described how people coped with war. Reading about fictional characters helped readers cope in real life.

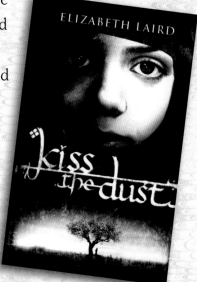

ELIZABETH LAIRD

▲
Kiss the Dust by Elizabeth Laird is set in Iraq in the 1980s. A Kurdish family, suspected of fighting against the Iraqi government, has to flee into the mountains of Iran. As refugees, they are not safe anywhere.

The words *serial* and *cereal* are homophones. Homophones are more common than you might think. The following homophones appear on this page: *by* (*buy*), *their* (*there, they're*), *great* (*grate*), *wrote* (*rote*), and *real* (*reel*).

Writing for Children

Scene from *Peter Pan* by J. M. Barrie

Before the 1700s, there were very few books written specifically for children. The books that did exist were written to teach something, such as the alphabet.

Illustration became an important part of children's literature in the 1800s. Illustrations can help the reader **visualize** the stories. The illustrations of fictional characters, such as Peter Pan and Alice in Wonderland, are as famous as the stories in which they appeared.

In the early 1900s, the first picture books were published. Beatrix Potter wrote very simple stories, such as *The Tale of Peter Rabbit* in 1901. Her books combined illustrations and only a few words to tell the story. In some picture books, the story is told entirely through the illustrations.

SHOCKER

The Very Hungry Caterpillar by Eric Carle was published in 1969. It is so popular that a copy is sold about every 57 seconds!

In 1957, a writer named Dr. Seuss was **commissioned** to write and illustrate a book. The author was asked to use no more than 250 words from a list of recommended vocabulary for beginning readers. *The Cat in the Hat* was born! In the end, Dr. Seuss used only 223 different words, but that was not an easy task. The book took several months to write. Did you know that Dr. Seuss was not a doctor at all? His real name was Theodor Seuss Geisel.

In the twentieth century, the importance of books for education increased. This meant that nonfiction for children also became popular. Magazines for children appeared. Some featured stories and comic strips. Others covered science or history topics.

Today, writers for children try to use interesting details and imaginative descriptions. They provide lively stories and cover important subjects.

◄ *Where the Wild Things Are* is an award-winning children's picture book. The characters in the book are brought to life through a combination of words and pictures. Maurice Sendak wrote and illustrated the book.

Progress in Children's Books

- before 1700 – very few books for children
- 1800s – more illustrations
- early 1900s – picture books become popular
- 2000s and today – more topics, educational

WHO ARE THEY?

Not all writers put their real name on the cover of a book. There are many reasons for this. They might just want to hide their identity. Writers who have other jobs as well as writing might not want it to be known that they are also an author.

PSEUDONYM:
LEMONY SNICKET
REAL NAME:
DANIEL HANDLER

A hundred years ago, it was often difficult for women to have their work published. If a woman used a man's name, she had a better chance of success. She was also more likely to be taken seriously. In nineteenth-century England, a writer named Mary Ann Evans published her novels under the **pseudonym** George Eliot. Her novels, including *Middlemarch*, were considered great works before and after her identity was discovered.

Not all women in the nineteenth century found it hard to get published. For example, the American writer Louisa May Alcott lived from 1832 to 1888. Some of her most well-known books were for older children. They include *Little Women*, and the sequel, *Good Wives*. Louisa used her pseudonym of A. M. Barnard for the books she wrote for adults.

PSEUDONYM:
  A. M. BARNARD
REAL NAME:
  LOUISA MAY ALCOTT

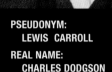

PSEUDONYM:
  LEWIS CARROLL
REAL NAME:
  CHARLES DODGSON

PSEUDONYM:
  GEORGE ELIOT
REAL NAME:
  MARY ANN EVANS

A famous recent pseudonym is Lemony Snicket. Lemony Snicket is the name on the cover of the books A Series of Unfortunate Events. The author's real name is Daniel Handler.

◀ Count Olaf, a main character in Snicket's books, as he appeared in a movie version of *A Series of Unfortunate Events.*

Pseudonym was a new word for me. The definition helped me understand. Also, once I began reading, the meaning became clearer. There is usually more than one way to figure out new words.

Book Ingredient: SEQUEL

A sequel is a book that continues from a previous book. Sequels usually feature the same characters. Some authors plan to write more than one book from the start. Others are asked to write another if their first book is a success.

GETTING PUBLISHED

Once a book is written, the next challenge is to get it published.
There are book publishers all over the world. Every day, publishers
receive many manuscripts from hopeful authors. Not all manuscripts
are published. The publishers have to choose those they think
are best, and those they believe will sell.
If you are submitting a manuscript,
you have to keep your fingers crossed!

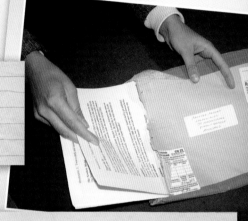

STAGE 1:

The author finishes writing. He or she sends
the manuscript to publishing companies.

STAGE 2:

The publisher receives the manuscript. Not all
submitted manuscripts are read at this stage.
A manuscript that is selected to be read is given
to the commissioning editor. He or she will read
it closely. It may be discussed with other editors.
If it is good enough, it will be published.

STAGE 3:

At this point, an editor will work on the book. He or
she will make decisions about who the readers are
likely to be and adjust the style of the book accordingly.
The editor will decide what size to make the book. The
author may be asked to make some changes to improve
the book. A designer will work on the layout of the
book and on the cover.

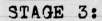

STAGE 4:

If the book is to be illustrated, the layout is given to an illustrator to produce pictures for the inside of the book. The illustrator may also work on the cover. Some books have photographs instead of illustrations. A photo researcher will look for the right photos.

STAGE 5:

The final manuscript is turned into a document that can be sent to a printer. Sending a book to be printed is called sending it to press. The word *press* is short for "printing press."

STAGE 6:

The book is printed and released by the publisher to bookstores. On a specific day, the book goes on sale.

SHOCKER

Writer's block is an author's nightmare. Instead of typing on a computer, or scribbling on paper, the writer cannot write. Whatever he or she does, no inspiration or ideas come to mind. Writer's block may end a writer's career!

Many books have been turned into movies. Sometimes people know about works of fiction only through the film version. Is seeing the film anything like reading the book? Can it be as good as reading, or replace the need to read the book? A film is usually a short version of the book. Things are left out, and changes have to be made.

WHAT DO YOU THINK?

Is watching the movie version of a book as good as reading the book?

PRO

I think that watching a movie is just as good. You can understand the story and characters. Sometimes the director's work can make you understand more than reading on your own. Movies sometimes set historical stories in the present day. This can help you understand the issues better.

When you watch a movie, you have to take the director's interpretation. Reading is a different activity from watching a movie. Most people read alone and quietly. You have to picture the scene and the characters. Reading can help broaden your vocabulary. It can also help you improve your own writing.

Movie characters from The Lord of the Rings

CON

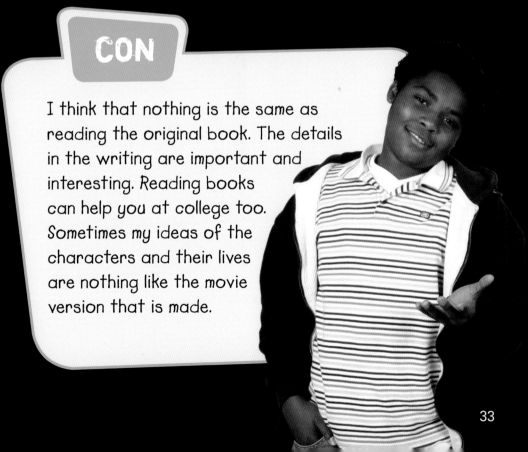

I think that nothing is the same as reading the original book. The details in the writing are important and interesting. Reading books can help you at college too. Sometimes my ideas of the characters and their lives are nothing like the movie version that is made.

GLOSSARY

Arma virumque cano, Troiae qui primus ab oris- Italium, fato profugus. Latin lavini aque venit- litora, multum ille et terris iactatus et alto - vi superum saevae memo- rem Iunonis ob iram; multa quoque et bello passus, dum conderet urbem, infer retque deos Latio, genus unde Latinum, Albanique patres, atque altae moenia Romae. Musa, mihi causas memora, quo numinae laeso, quidve dolens, regina deum tot adire labores impulerit. Tantaene ani mis caelestibus irae? Urbs antiqua fuit, Ty ryii tenuere coloni, Karthago, Italiam cont ra Tiberinaque longe ostia, dives opum studiisque asperrima belli; quam Iuono fertur terris magis omnibus unam post habita colluisse Samo; hic illius arma, hic currus fuit: hoc regnum dea gentibus esse si qua fata sinant, iam tum tenditkque. fovetque. Progeniem sed enim iulia Troiano,

Calligraphy

annex an extra part of a building that is joined onto or placed near the main building

biography a book that tells someone's life story

Braille a system of writing for blind people, using raised dots that can be felt with the fingers

calligraphy the art of beautiful handwriting

clone to grow an animal or a plant from the cells of a parent plant or animal so that it is identical to the parent

commission to offer someone money to do a specific task

controversial (*con truh VER shuhl*) causing a great deal of argument or disagreement

dictate to talk aloud so that your words can be written down

distort to twist or change things so that the truth or facts are hidden

fable a story that teaches a lesson

folktale a story that is passed down orally through generations

myth (*MITH*) a traditional story that expresses beliefs or a world view

nonfiction writing that gives information about real things

novel a book that tells a story about made-up people and events

pamphleteer a person who writes short political or social texts

parchment a heavy, paper-like material made from animal skin

patent (*PAT uhnt*) a legal document giving an inventor sole rights over his or her invention

playwright a person who writes plays

Renaissance (*REN uh sahnts*) the period in European history that began in Italy in about 1300 and lasted until about 1600

slander information made public that is damaging to someone's reputation

trilogy a set of three related works

visualize (*VIZH oo hu lize*) to picture something in your mind

FIND OUT MORE

BOOKS

Carpenter, Angelica Shirley. *Lewis Carroll: Through the Looking Glass*. Lerner Publishing Group, 2003.

Coren, Michael. *J. R. R. Tolkien: The Man Who Created the Lord of the Rings*. Scholastic, 2001.

Dahl, Roald. *Boy: Tales of Childhood*. Puffin Books, 1999.

Heinrichs, Ann. *The Printing Press*. Franklin Watts, 2005.

Kovacs, Deborah. *Meet the Authors: 25 Writers of Upper Elementary and Middle School Books Talk About Their Work*. Scholastic Inc., 1999.

Strom, Laura Layton. *Mirror Power*. Scholastic Inc., 2008.

WEB SITES

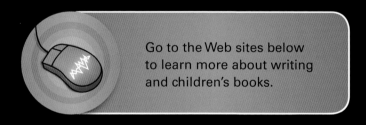

Go to the Web sites below to learn more about writing and children's books.

www.factmonster.com/ipka/A0768701.html

www.kidsonthenet.com

www.roalddahl.com

www.jkrowling.com

www.seussville.com

INDEX

ABOUT THE AUTHOR

Jennifer Murray, whenever she can, likes to curl up on her sofa and read a book. She sometimes skips doing chores or reads late into the night if she is reading something exciting. For as long as she can remember, Jennifer has loved reading all kinds of fiction and nonfiction books. She always has a book in her bag just in case there is time to stop and read a chapter or two!